DILEMMAS IN DEMOCRACY

Fake News and Propaganda

Fiona Young-Brown

Cavendish Square
New York

Published in 2020 by Cavendish Square Publishing, LLC
243 5th Avenue, Suite 136, New York, NY 10016

First Edition

Website: cavendishsq.com

Library of Congress Cataloging-in-Publication Data

Names: Young-Brown, Fiona, author.
Title: Fake news and propaganda / Fiona Young-Brown.
Description: First edition. | New York : Cavendish Square, 2019. |
Series: Dilemmas in democracy | Includes bibliographical references and index.
Identifiers: LCCN 2018054579 (print) | LCCN 2018060630 (ebook) | ISBN 9781502644978 (ebook) | ISBN 9781502644961 (library bound) | ISBN 9781502644954 (pbk.)
Subjects: LCSH: Fake news--United States--Juvenile literature |
Propaganda--United States--Juvenile literature. | Press and politics--United States.
Classification: LCC PN4888.F35 (ebook) | LCC PN4888.F35 Y68 2019 (print) |
DDC 070.4/3--dc23
LC record available at https://lccn.loc.gov/2018054579

Editorial Director: David McNamara
Editor: Caitlyn Miller
Copy Editor: Alex Tessman
Associate Art Director: Alan Sliwinski
Designer: Christina Shults
Production Coordinator: Karol Szymczuk
Photo Research: J8 Media

The photographs in this book are used by permission and through the courtesy of:
Cover yellowline/Shutterstock.com; background (and used throughout the book) Artist Elizaveta/Shutterstock.com; p. 4 Pool/Getty Images; p. 6 iPhone/Alamy Stock Photo; pp. 8-9 Chris Hellier/Alamy Stock Photo; p. 11 Photo 12/Alamy Stock Photo; p. 15 Jeff Kravitz/FilmMagic, Inc/Getty Images; p. 17 Imagno/Hulton Archive/Getty Images; pp. 22-23 Rob Crandall/Shutterstock.com; pp. 26, 29, 68 The Washington Post/Getty Images; p. 31 dennizn/Shutterstock.com; p. 35 Universal History Archive/Universal Images Group/Getty Images; p. 37 ©Ad Fontes Media, Inc.; pp. 38-39 Joseph Sohm/Shuterstock.com; p. 40 Mandel Ngan/AFP/Getty Images; p. 44 Chesnot/Getty Images; p. 47 Alexandros Michailidis/Shutterstock.com; p. 48 Bloomberg/Getty Images; p. 51 A_Lesik/Shutterstock.com; p. 52 Carl Court/Getty Images; p. 56 Richard Levine/Alamy Stock Photo; p. 59 Sharaf Maksumov/Shutterstock.com; p. 60 Xinhua News Agency/Getty Images; p. 63 Mark Wilson/Getty Images; pp. 64-65 Chris Rogers/Photolibrary/Getty Images.

Printed in the United States of America

CONTENTS

laying its foundation on such principles and organizing
form, as to them shall seem most likely to effect their Safety and
indeed, will dictate that Governments long established
for light and transient causes; and accordingly all experience
to suffer, while evils are sufferable than to
to which they are accustomed. But when a
pursuing invariably the same Object evinces a
Despotism, it is their right, it is their duty, to
new Guards for their future security.

CHAPTER 1

What Are Fake News and Propaganda?

Since the 2016 US presidential election, one phrase seems to appear everywhere: fake news. It is discussed on television, in conversations, and in political campaigns. It is a widespread problem. In fact, experts believe that the average American saw at least one fake news story in the months immediately before the 2016 election. Of those who did see a fake news story, more than half of them believed those stories to be true.

But what is fake news? Is the idea really new? Is it different from propaganda, and if so, how? Perhaps most importantly, are fake news and propaganda dangerous?

Defining Fake News

Fake news can be defined in a variety of ways, but the simplest definition is the most accurate. It is any news story that contains false information on purpose. Or, to quote librarian

Opposite: Hillary Clinton and Donald Trump debate during the 2016 presidential election. The 2016 election was when the term "fake news" first became widely used.

The *Onion* is a well-known satirical website. Satire is a form of fake news.

and author Donald Barclay, "Fake news is really just the latest name for the ancient art of lying."

Fake news can take many forms and can have many different goals, some harmless, some less so. For example, satire can be a form of fake news. The *Onion*, which bills itself as "America's Finest News Source," is a satirical publication that pokes fun at the real news. Recent stories include one about a study claiming to have discovered that more than five million birds die every year after colliding with clouds. It doesn't take much time to realize that the story is obviously false and written for entertainment purposes. A story like this is one example of fake news.

Another goal of fake news, besides entertainment, is to make money. After the 2016 election, investigations found that people in several villages in Eastern Europe had made a large amount of money by creating and spreading fake news stories. This is where the intention of fake news becomes a little murkier. The stories being spread were not all obviously false, and while they made money, they also served another purpose—as propaganda.

Propaganda is a form of fake news. Sometimes, it may have a significant amount of truth to it. The key is that propaganda is designed to manipulate people's emotions and to win them over to support a particular political agenda. Even propaganda can be difficult to spot at times. After all, what one person believes to be propaganda may be accepted as the truth by someone else.

Historical Examples

Despite their recent rise to prominence, neither fake news nor propaganda are particularly new. The ancient Greeks used plays as a form of propaganda in order to manipulate people's responses to an event by using popular culture. Through theatrical performance,

Greek plays were an early form of propaganda, used to calm or to rile up the public about an issue.

they could get the public riled up about an issue or calm them down about a social upheaval. In other words, the writer could manipulate the way people felt about an issue by deciding how to "spin" the story. This is no different from how modern television and radio broadcasts, newspapers, and magazines often work. The creator brings a certain bias on a topic to present it in a certain light.

The Voice of America is an international radio service funded by the US government that has been broadcast in various parts of the world since 1942. It was first used during the Second World War to transmit war news and patriotic songs through Europe and the Pacific. During the Cold War, it started broadcasting to Communist countries with a pro-American message designed to fight anti-American propaganda. Later, Arabic transmissions were sent when tensions were rising in the Middle East. The intent of these broadcasts was to show America in a positive light and to promote the Western ideal of freedom. Meanwhile, other broadcasts were operated by Japanese and German sources to promote an opposing view. In many ways, this was not so different from the ancient Greeks and their theatrical performances.

Such broadcasts aren't limited to times of war. There are some who would argue that audiences are continually exposed to propaganda in one form or another through something as simple as television entertainment. The US Navy was heavily involved in the production of the 1986 movie *Top Gun*, which would make sense to help the film's accuracy. After the movie was released, recruitment in the Navy increased dramatically. Could this count as propaganda? Since the 2001 World Trade Center attacks, there have been dozens of new television dramas about government agencies: *NCIS*, *FBI*, *Homeland*, and so on. Are they pure entertainment or are they intended to encourage public faith in the government?

Propaganda was widely used during World War II. This Japanese poster was created in 1941 to criticize the US president.

Arguments could be made either way, emphasizing that propaganda is not always obvious.

Both fake news and propaganda can be more easily spread when media is made more readily and cheaply available to the public. The mid to late nineteenth century saw a rise in fake news stories in the United States. It was easy and cheap to begin production of a newspaper, and so many towns, political groups, and ethnic communities all started their own weeklies or dailies. On the one hand, this was a good thing. It brought news of current events to the masses. Yet there was also a downside. Each publication was aimed at a specific audience and so typically took on a partisan tone to give them what they wanted to hear. Fact-checking took a back seat to pleasing and entertaining one's readership. Even one town might have a dozen different newspapers in a dozen different languages, each for one ethnic group, meaning that people read only what suited their specific perspective.

In the twentieth century, this ease of reaching an audience took several forms. First radio became readily available, and then television followed. Some argued that this was the start of stories being reduced to sound bites. An on-air journalist's success relied on their charisma and personality. Now social media and the internet have once again made distribution even easier and cheaper. It has allowed for the rise of so-called citizen journalists, providing a means for anyone, anywhere to put out a story and share it with a broad audience.

While one positive of citizen journalism is that groups that may have typically been ignored now have a voice, it also carries a downside. It is now all too easy to create and distribute a story that has no editing, no fact-checking, and no filtering. Accuracy has slipped to the background, and a story can go viral without any hard evidence to support it. Fake news may not be new, but technology has allowed for its influence to grow in ways previously unimagined.

In short, fake news is a story that is intentionally false. It may be purely for entertainment purposes; it may be to make money; or it may be to intentionally mislead an audience and manipulate their response to a topic. The latter can also be known as propaganda. However, the term "fake news" has come to mean much more than its original meaning, and it is important to understand this. All too often, the phrase is now thrown about to refer to anything the audience or the story's subject does not *want* to be true. Rather than respond to a story that is critical of someone's actions, it has become much more common to simply dismiss it as fake news.

Propaganda as a Positive Tool

Despite the fact that the term "propaganda" is often seen in a negative light, it can be used for good. Before exploring some of the dangers of fake news or propaganda, here's a look at some of the positives.

Some of the most obvious benefits of propaganda can be seen in times of war. Propaganda allows a government to shape a conflict in a way that builds national pride and support. It also allows them to keep some information hidden for the protection of the public. News broadcasts shown in the United States and Britain during the Second World War would show footage of the fighting overseas that had been edited and narrated in such a manner that the spirits of the audience would be kept high. Patriotic slogans and messages that said victory was near helped to keep the public engaged and energized to contribute to the war effort.

In a similar fashion, after the September 11 attacks on New York's World Trade Center in 2001, news stories were often mixed with inspirational portraits of the first responders and the survivors. People were shown reminders that America was not a nation to bow in cowardice and that the country would recover to be even stronger and better. This was a form of propaganda, designed to raise public morale by stressing a positive national character. It worked, too, as was evident in the increased number of flags and symbols of national pride that were on display following the attacks. Not that this rise in national pride was without its negatives. It also led to an increase in negative propaganda about Muslims and anyone viewed as "other." Propaganda can be a double-edged sword.

Propaganda is also often used in advertising. Marketing materials are intended to shape our opinions in much the same way that political propaganda is. Sometimes there may be a very fine line between the two.

Marketing or Propaganda?

In 1990, Virgin America started a campaign to encourage young people to take an interest in politics and to vote. Still in operation, Rock the Vote has used popular singers and Hollywood stars to raise awareness through advertising on MTV (a partner of the program) and social media. In 1996, Rock the Vote created the first telephone voter registration system, and then the first online voter registration system. The program described itself as nonpartisan and said their goal was to emphasize the importance of voting. However, some people might argue that over the years, the lines between a simple voter registration drive and political partisanship have become blurred.

Rock the Vote has publicly supported President Obama's Affordable Care Act. More recently, the program has supported such issues as gun control, the legalization of marijuana, and environmental protections. While Rock the Vote argues that these are nonpartisan issues that affect everyone, their work has drawn criticism from members of the Republican Party. Many Republicans say that this support of progressive issues makes Rock the Vote little more than liberal propaganda.

It certainly seems that the line may have been crossed during the 2004 presidential election when Rock the Vote sent fake draft

Rock the Vote's claims to be nonpartisan have been criticized by some who see the campaign as only promoting liberal issues.

notices to more than six hundred thousand people. The messages, complete with a copy of the Republican defense secretary's signature, told recipients that they had been drafted to vote. Whether the intent was innocent or not, the messages did result in a higher voter turnout among young voters in areas where they were distributed. Rock the Vote has also started a Democracy Class program to teach high school students about voting and elections.

Movie Propaganda During the Second World War

During the Second World War, propaganda played an important part on both sides, and one of the easiest ways to reach a large number of people was through movies.

In 1933, Adolf Hitler established the Ministry of Enlightenment and Propaganda. The ministry's purpose was to influence and mold public opinion. They were very successful in doing so. German filmmaker Leni Riefenstahl made a number of films promoting the Nazi regime and praising the successes of the Germans at the 1936 Olympics. Other films were decidedly anti-Semitic in nature. Jewish people were portrayed as less than human. Such propaganda helped to fuel the anti-Jewish sentiment that would eventually lead to the horrors of the Holocaust.

Meanwhile, in the United States, nationalist propaganda was also being shared with audiences, but it was considered part of the war effort and was produced by the Office of War Information. The Office of Strategic Services, founded in 1942, issued a memo that "the motion picture is one of the most powerful propaganda weapons at the disposal of the United States." Movies emphasized American values and patriotism while showing Germans, Italians, and Japanese as subhuman villains. They were designed to strengthen public support for the troops fighting overseas.

German filmmaker Leni Riefenstahl created a number of pro-Nazi propaganda films during the 1930s. Shown here is the premiere of *Triumph of the Will* (1935).

Is this an example of a successful marketing campaign to raise awareness of issues and civic participation? Or is it a form of propaganda? Arguments could certainly be made both ways. It is worth remembering that something is often labeled propaganda by those who oppose its message. Propaganda and advertising both seek to create some form of emotional response, and that is not always a negative. For example, the propaganda shown to Americans during the Second World War was intended to build a sense of courage and pride. Whereas advertising sets out to convince its audience that they want a specific product or service, propaganda intends to convert them to a particular set of ideals or political position.

The Negative Side of Propaganda

Although it can be used for good, more often than not propaganda can be seen as negative. Returning to the example of the Second World War, propaganda was used to incite and justify genocide (the mass killing of a group of people). Adolf Hitler wanted to promote the notion that Germans were the so-called master race. To do this, he ordered the production of materials that praised the Aryan ideal: people who were tall, blonde, and blue-eyed (even though Hitler himself did not fit this image). However, if one race was superior, others must be "less than" or subhuman.

Anyone of a different background was singled out by Hitler and the Nazis. Eastern Europeans, including Slavs, Poles, and Romani, were looked down upon and subject to discrimination and imprisonment. Those subjected to the worst cruelty were the

Jewish people. Posters, films, and newspaper articles depicted them as sinister, greedy, and dangerous.

Hitler said that the only way for the master race to thrive was to remove this "threat" from society. Anti-Semitic propaganda in wartime Germany was enormously successful, tragically so. It built upon existing prejudices and caused them to rise to fever pitch. At the same time, it also created fear. Many Germans, even if they did not agree with the campaign, turned a blind eye, thankful that it was not them being targeted. This propaganda, fear, and hatred led to mass genocide. No definitive numbers exist, but it is estimated that six million Jews were murdered (as well as several million Slavs, Romani, Eastern Europeans, and people with disabilities).

While it might be tempting to believe that such a horror could never happen again, propaganda has been misused to promote war much more recently. The US invasion of Iraq was justified by the argument that the nation was in possession of weapons of mass destruction. Anti-Muslim sentiment made people more willing to accept such an argument, and American troops were deployed in 2003. It was later revealed that there were no such weapons and the invasion had been based upon false information. Some might argue that this didn't matter. After all, dictator Saddam Hussein was overthrown.

However, between 2003 and 2011, when troops withdrew, several thousand American soldiers had been killed, as many as a million wounded, and an estimated five hundred thousand Iraqi people had been killed. Once the American people learned they'd been misled, there was also a massive loss of confidence in the American government.

The United Nations Speaks Out Against Fake News

Several branches of the United Nations (UN) have spoken out against the increasing use of politically motivated fake news and propaganda.

In 2017, the UN noted that there had been an alarming rise in the amount of fake news. David Kaye is the current Special Rapporteur on Freedom of Opinion and Expression, a role within the Human Rights Council. In 2017, he issued a Joint Declaration with members of the Organization for Security and Co-operation in Europe (OSCE), the Organization of American States (OAS), and the African Commission on Human and Peoples' Rights (ACHPR). The declaration warned that state actors (i.e., national leaders, politicians, etc.) should not "make, sponsor, encourage, or further disseminate statements which they know or reasonably should know to be false (disinformation) or which demonstrate a reckless disregard for verifiable information (propaganda)."

The declaration placed the responsibility on people in power to ensure that they did not spread false information. The UN also expressed concerns about the possibility of censorship as a means to reduce fake news, saying, "There is a risk that efforts to counter it could lead to censorship, the suppression of critical thinking and other approaches contrary to human rights law."

Elsewhere in the United Nations, the focus has turned to helping journalists combat the spread of fake news. The International Program for the Development of Communication (IPDC) was launched as part of the United Nations Educational, Scientific, and Cultural Organization (UNESCO) in the 1980s. Its original purpose was to help promote and strengthen the development of a free media in developing nations. More recently, the organization has also turned its attention to fake news. In 2018, IPDC released an

David Kaye is the UN Rapporteur on Freedom of Opinion and Expression.

in-depth report that journalists can use as a training resource. Topics covered include the importance of truth in journalism, the different types of misinformation and how they can be spread, information literacy, fact-checking, and dealing with abuse.

The United Nations has spoken out about the problem of intentional fake news. The solution, they argue, is not to make laws or carry out censorship that may further stifle free speech. Rather, they emphasize the need to raise the standards of journalism and to educate the public so that attempts to mislead can be more easily spotted and ignored.

Fake news became a key topic during the 2016 US presidential election, and disinformation is thought to have heavily influenced some voters.

VOTE

A Threat to Democracy

Many experts now say that the rise of so much fake news and propaganda is a threat to democracy. Fake news, when used for obvious entertainment purposes and nothing more, may be harmless, as is some propaganda. However, the downside is that both can be used to erode trust and to build suspicion of those with a different mindset. This can have potentially dangerous consequences.

PEN International is an organization that promotes the freedom of expression through writing. They argue that freedom of expression is essential to a thriving democracy. If that is the case, fake news might not sound like a bad thing. However, fake news can damage access to democracy. Although once used to refer to stories that are obviously false, the term "fake news" has now become a political weapon that is used to silence anyone who offers an opposing or critical point of view. While the term is thrown about by all areas of the political spectrum, a study by the Internet Institute at Oxford University found that the majority of actual fake news came from right-wing sources.

Journalists have warned that this points to a dangerous breakdown of political debate. Instead of creating reasonable discussions, the press is labeled un-American when it publishes anything critical of the government. Indeed, President Trump has referred to the American media as "the enemy of the people." The United Nations High Commissioner for Human Rights, Zeid Ra'ad al-Hussein, has responded to this: "To call these news organizations fake does tremendous damage. I believe it could amount to incitement."

For a democracy to thrive, freedom of expression must be protected, but so must the ability to discuss and debate issues. Information is vital, and people must have access to accurate information so that they can make educated decisions. It can be argued that the rise in fake news, especially such as that seen during and since the 2016 US presidential election, is a deliberate attempt to destroy public faith in journalism. It encourages people not to believe what they read in the newspaper but to seek out only that information that supports their viewpoint. This leads to a state of hyper-partisanship. People become more convinced their viewpoint is entirely correct and anything else is dangerous.

Democracy is about more than being able to vote. It is about having access to the information that allows you to make an educated decision when you vote. A free press helps to support an educated voting population. When that free press is silenced through threats of being fake, it is not just information that is distorted, but democracy. A person cannot vote in a truly democratic fashion if they are only permitted certain information.

PIZZAGATE
IS
NOT
FAKE
NEWS
INVESTIGATE
PIZZAGATE

CHAPTER 2

Fake News and Propaganda in Modern America

In April 1844, the *New York Sun* told of the first exciting crossing of the Atlantic in a balloon. In just seventy-five hours, Mr. Monck Mason and Mr. Harrison Ainsworth had floated from the Bristol Channel to the coast of North America, and they had recorded the entire event in their diary. There was just one problem. The story was a hoax.

The balloon crossing was a work of fiction by renowned author Edgar Allan Poe, but it was reported as if it were an actual event. (The first balloon to cross the Atlantic wouldn't do so until 1978). All in all, the hoax was harmless, a piece of entertainment that helped to sell a lot of newspapers. Fake news stories such as these were relatively common, helping one newspaper outsell another.

Not all fake news stories were as benign. Some are believed to have started a war. In the 1890s, newspaper magnates William Randolph Hearst and Joseph Pulitzer were locked in a bitter battle for readership. Each was constantly trying

Opposite: Fake news stories such as "Pizzagate" spread far and wide in the modern age of social media.

to outdo the other, and making up stories was no obstacle. At the time, tensions were running high between Spain and Cuba, and the United States was interested in obtaining Cuba.

Hearst had sent an artist to the island to capture pictures of the events, but when he arrived, things were quite calm. The artist sent a telegram to Hearst to say that tensions had died down. Hearst's alleged response was, "You furnish the pictures and I'll furnish the war." Shortly afterward, the USS *Maine* sank in Havana harbor following an explosion. The cause was not known, but Hearst and his rivals quickly labeled it an act of aggression by the Spanish. The level of public outcry they managed to create was enormous. More than two hundred American sailors had been killed. The resulting Spanish-American War is considered by many historians to be the first press-driven war. Fake news had played a large part in starting the conflict.

Modern Fake News

In recent decades, there have been several notable cases where journalists have been revealed as frauds who made up their stories. A story in the *Washington Post* in 1980 told of an eight-year-old heroin addict. The author won a Pulitzer Prize for her reporting, which was quickly discovered to be fake. In 1998, a writer for the *New Republic* admitted to having made up an estimated two-thirds of the stories he had written for the magazine, while a respected writer at the *New York Times* was exposed in 2003 for having been making up stories and quotes since his time at a college newspaper. These revelations of fake news were all considered shocking, though news brokers of the past such as Hearst and even Pulitzer might well have said that the writers were giving both readers and publishers what they wanted. However, in doing so, they greatly damaged the

The fake Pizzagate story eventually led to a gunman threatening staff at a pizza restaurant. Here, community members show support for the people affected by the dangerous story.

reputation of journalism, which relies on an underlying assumption of truth.

Other examples of fake news have been more directly dangerous. During the 2016 US election cycle, a story started online that claimed the Democratic Party was behind a large child-trafficking network. The claim was spread, with additional lies being added. Soon the *Conservative Daily Post* was reporting that the FBI had confirmed raiding the home of presidential candidate Hillary Clinton. Both the alleged raid and the FBI statement were false. Right-wing fake news sites repeated the conspiracy until it reached fever pitch. Conspiracy theorists claimed to know code words being used by those involved in the trafficking of children and that a pizza restaurant in Washington, DC, was a front for the scheme. The restaurant's staff were harassed and threatened.

Finally, in December 2016, a man walked into the restaurant and fired several shots, claiming that he was there to rescue the (nonexistent) children. Fortunately, no one was hurt. The *New York Times*, the *Washington Post*, and several other major newspapers all debunked the conspiracy theory. Pizzagate, as the theory became known, remains an example of the dangers that a fake news story can create.

Elsewhere, additional false claims against Hillary Clinton included her selling weapons to terrorist group ISIS and her being linked to the murder of an FBI agent. Meanwhile, in a fake headline, Pope Francis gave an overwhelming endorsement of Donald Trump.

Adding to the problem of fake news has been what many journalists view as a crusade against the free press by President Trump. During his presidency, he has frequently made comments on Twitter about the media being un-American and an enemy of the people. He has repeatedly labeled any media that is critical of him as fake news, and so the term has been warped. Now, fake news can mean anything that is critical of a certain point of view, often causing actual fake news to be overlooked. This is another form of propaganda, or an attempt to manipulate what people believe. As President Trump told one reporter, "I do it to discredit you all and demean you all so that when you write negative stories about me no one will believe you."

Supermarket tabloids commonly spread absurd news stories.

This tactic appears to be working. Press conferences at the White House show an increasing hostility against members of some news outlets and praise for those who report favorably about the government. Lies remain unchallenged, and public confidence in journalists continues to decline.

A Gallup poll in 2015 found that the public's trust of the news media had sunk to a new low. With writers being exposed as frauds, there was a growing suspicion of mainstream media and journalistic integrity. Yet modern readers present something of a dilemma. They want real truthful news but often seek out and believe only that which confirms their individual beliefs. They think of everything else as untrustworthy. At the same time, the popularity of publications such as the *National Enquirer*, which clearly publish fake stories as entertainment, continues. Are readers able to spot

Does the Constitution Protect Against Fake News?

"Congress shall make no law respecting an establishment of religion, or prohibiting the free exercise thereof; or abridging the freedom of speech, or of the press; or the right of the people peaceably to assemble, and to petition the Government for a redress of grievances."

—Amendment 1, United States Constitution

The First Amendment is clear in its defense of free speech, and that also applies to a free press. However, there are some restrictions. (One example is that defamation is not protected as free speech.) Over time, courts have heard many cases related to the freedom of the press.

In 1931, the state of Minnesota tried to pass a law to prevent the publication of malicious news. The Supreme Court overturned the law as a violation of the First Amendment. Just a few years later, the Supreme Court described freedom of the press as "a fundamental personal right." Justice Louis Brandeis argued that these rights assume that there will be some false speech (or fake news). The answer, he said, was not censorship but "more speech." This opinion has since been repeated by many, although in 2003, the Supreme Court ruled that the First Amendment does not necessarily protect all speech when the intent is to threaten.

To ensure freedom of speech and freedom of the press means making sure that the public has access to more information. Therefore, the Constitution protects against fake news by allowing access to information, with the idea that information is the best weapon against propaganda.

the differences between fake news and real journalism? Or do they simply use the "fake news" criticism for things they dislike?

The lines between obvious fake news and true journalism have become increasingly blurred. As a result, many people now believe what they might read on a supermarket tabloid cover while dismissing a story in the *Washington Post* or the *New York Times*.

Repetition and Propaganda Techniques

Joseph Goebbels, minister of propaganda in Nazi Germany during the Second World War, once said, "A lie told once remains a lie, but a lie told a thousand times becomes the truth." This sums up the ways in which fake news and propaganda can be so effective in manipulating people's opinions. If you hear something once, you might not think much about it. But if you hear similar stories over and over, eventually your brain absorbs the information, and you start to think there must be a nugget of truth in it.

One example of this constant repetition of falsehoods to create a seed of doubt can be found in the tabloid press. Publications such as the *National Enquirer* and the *Globe* are known for their sensationalist, outrageous stories, and many people view them as little more than entertainment or gossip. However, during the 2016 US presidential election, their brand of falsehood took on a political tone. An overwhelming number of cover stories praised Republican candidate Donald Trump, while a similar number depicted Democratic candidate Hillary Clinton as criminal, suspect, or seriously ill. Even the mainstream media took note that these magazines seemed to be adopting a new role as a "propaganda arm" for certain political interests.

The tabloid press followed many of the classic steps in producing propaganda. The first step to producing propaganda is to put out as many falsehoods as possible. One lie isn't enough, but if enough lies are repeated, one is likely to eventually take root. There is no need for stories to be consistent to create propaganda. Rather, there should be enough of them that the public is overwhelmed by the sheer volume. And, of course, effective fake news should always have just enough facts to make the story believable.

How effective are such techniques? It can be difficult to measure accurately, but the importance of repeated exposure shouldn't be discounted. Grocery store tabloids often sell fewer than half a million copies of each issue. With these numbers, it is easy to consider them unimportant. However, they form a part of our popular culture. Although few copies are sold, they sit in every checkout aisle and are seen by hundreds of thousands of people every day. Without realizing it, we absorb the headlines repeatedly.

Russian Interference

Aside from tabloids, another source of fake news and propaganda comes from much farther away. Throughout the Cold War, Communist-controlled Russia made frequent use of propaganda to promote Russian society and to discredit the United States as a degenerate, failing nation. Often it was clumsy and easily recognizable. Now there is a new form of Russian propaganda. It is much subtler in its presentation, which is why it has been able to become so influential.

In 2018, a series of Congressional hearings revealed that Russians were behind thousands of fake social media accounts that had helped to spread fake news during the 2016 election cycle. Also, more than 3,500 ads had been placed on Facebook and Instagram by the Internet Research Agency (IRA). The organization has since been indicted by a US grand jury on charges of "violating criminal

This Soviet propaganda poster from 1955 warns Russians to remain alert, presumably for possible Western threats.

laws with the intent to interfere with US elections and political processes." In other words, the Justice Department believes they have tried to interfere with US democracy.

The IRA was founded in Saint Petersburg, Russia, in 2013. Apparently funded by their country's government, the organization's purpose is to use an online presence to manipulate media and popular opinion in ways that will benefit Russian interests. One way to do this is by creating online accounts and campaigns pretending to be social activists. They have focused on issues that already divide people and then seek to deepen those divides. For example, in the United States, the IRA ran propaganda campaigns related to gun control, immigration, and racial tensions, even going so far as to set up protests for the Black Lives Matter movement. These were and continue to be legitimate issues within the United States. However, the IRA was able to infiltrate groups such as Black Lives Matter to make existing tensions even worse and to feed a growing distrust of mainstream media. They did this by pretending, for example, to be a Black Lives Matter activist and then posting memes about supposed stories the mainstream media wouldn't report on.

In addition to posing within groups to incite tension, the IRA and other Russian propagandists have learned how to copy Western journalism. Old-style Soviet propaganda was very easy to spot, using language that obviously reflected Communist views. The new version of Russian media is stylistically similar and difficult to tell apart from any American news broadcast. This has made it easier to fool members of the public. It doesn't have the appearance of propaganda, so it has been able to subtly manipulate and sway public opinion.

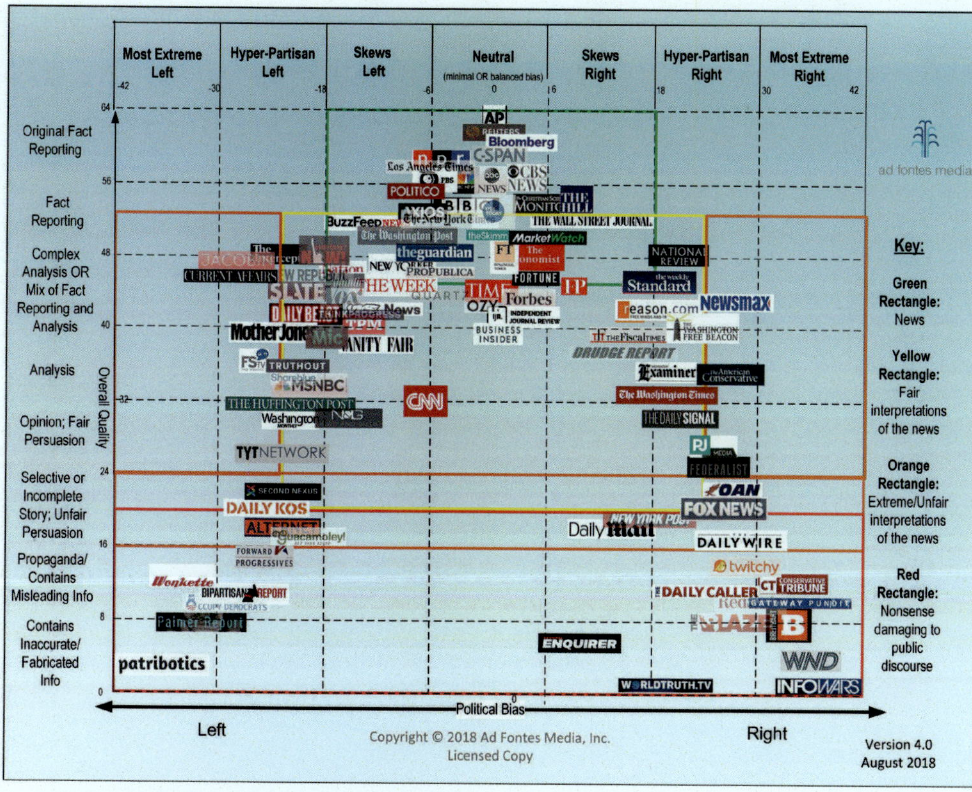

This chart attempts to highlight the various biases of major media outlets, noting political leanings and each publication's accuracy.

Bias in Mainstream Media

Despite claiming to be "fair and balanced," the media has always been accused of carrying some bias. Newspapers were published to appeal to certain audiences and so, over time, they framed the

It is believed that Russian agents infiltrated the Black Lives Matter movement to make existing racial tensions worse and to feed mistrust of the American media.

BLACK
LIVES
MATTER!

Journalists in Danger

In June 2018, an armed man shot and killed five people, including four journalists, at the *Capital Gazette* in Maryland.

Stories of journalists facing violence or imprisonment around the world are not particularly new. During the apartheid era in South Africa, many journalists faced jail for speaking out against the discriminatory practice. In fact, between 1992 and 2017, 1,279 journalists have been killed around the world. More than 800 of these were murdered.

For a long time, this kind of violence against the press has been associated with the Middle East or places where there has been a great deal of government upheaval and social unrest. However, since the 2016 US presidential election and the growing distrust of the media, threats of violence against journalists in the United States have risen.

On June 28, 2018, an armed man walked into the offices of the *Capital Gazette* in Annapolis, Maryland, and opened fire. He killed five people, four of whom were journalists. The gunman had been involved in a lawsuit against the newspaper, but many believe that anti-media comments by some politicians had further incited violence. Four months later, a series of pipe bombs were delivered to a number of liberal targets, including the offices of broadcaster CNN. Fortunately, the packages were intercepted, and no one was harmed. Stirring anti-media feelings can have deadly consequences.

news in ways that would satisfy that desire. Even as far back as 1807, Thomas Jefferson warned of the risk of fake news:

> *To your request of my opinion of the manner in which a newspaper should be conducted so as to be most useful, I should answer "by restraining it to true facts & sound principles only." yet I fear such a paper would find few subscribers ... nothing can now be believed which is seen in a newspaper.*

As news outlets spread to radio, and then television, and now the internet, accusations of bias have become more widespread. It is generally accepted that different news stations follow certain political lines. In fact, a chart is regularly updated showing where on the political spectrum each outlet falls and what level of complex analysis and truthful interpretation they provide. Among those outlets considered most balanced and accurate in their reporting are many of the major brands such as the *New York Times*, the *Washington Post*, NPR, CBS, Reuters, and so on. At the opposite end of the spectrum, falling within the categories of extreme partisan bias and publishing "nonsense that is damaging to public discourse" are such titles as the *National Enquirer*, InfoWars, Palmer Report, and Fox News.

The motto of Fox News used to be "fair and balanced," a claim that drew much criticism from liberal consumers. In June 2017, they announced a new slogan: "Most Watched, Most Trusted." Just a few months later, it changed to "Real News, Real Honest Opinion." The station has had a reputation for being conservative in its bias for a long time. With the rise of fake news, they have been a vocal supporter of President Trump calling the mainstream media “fake news.”

However, multiple studies show that Fox News is responsible for a large number of fake news stories. PolitiFact, a fact-checking service that rates outlets for accuracy, concludes that statements made on the channel were mostly false to “pants on fire” false 59 percent of the time. Other studies have argued that viewers who get most of their news coverage from Fox are often the least informed on many major topics such as climate change or international affairs. The studies have been dismissed by Fox hosts as propaganda.

CNN is often accused of being at the opposite end of the political spectrum from Fox, and MediaBias rates the network as left-wing in its leanings. However, an analysis of recent statements found that its claims were false about 26 percent of the time. Although this is significantly less than Fox, and although conservative outlets have been shown to provide more fake news stories, it should not be assumed that more liberal press outlets are automatically more truthful. Even some outlets considered balanced and neutral such as CBS have been found to have a false rating of 45 percent. So despite claims to be fighting fake news, all too often, mainstream media outlets are responsible for sharing much of it.

CHAPTER 3

Disinformation on a Global Scale

The problem of fake news is not limited to the United States. Fake news and political propaganda are becoming an increasing threat to democracies around the world. As a result, many countries have been struggling to decide how best to deal with it.

France

Fake news reared its head during the 2017 election for the French presidency. A series of online rumors targeted candidate Emmanuel Macron with allegations that he had a hidden bank account in the Bahamas so that he could avoid paying taxes. After his opponent, Marine Le Pen, repeated the claims in a televised debate, Macron responded that he would be filing a defamation lawsuit. The rumors, complete with images of apparent bank documents, appeared on a web forum that had been known to spread a lot of fake stories during the 2016 US election cycle. The story was soon debunked, and

Opposite: Fake news is a global problem. During the 2017 French presidential election, eventual winner Emmanuel Macron (shown here) was targeted by fake news stories.

the images were proven to be false, but not until it had been shared extensively on social media. Another candidate had been targeted during earlier rounds of voting. A false story linked him to the Muslim Brotherhood. Anti-Muslim sentiments were running high in France, and so the story was an obvious attempt to manipulate these views to discredit him.

Macron went on to win the presidency. Several months later he announced that he was writing a couple of bills to fight future instances of fake news. Drafts of the bills were released in 2018 to much debate. The proposed laws would protect against "the manipulation of information" in the three months immediately before an election. If the new legislation were enacted, a political candidate would have the right to ask the courts to stop the publication of any information that might be fake. Judges would be given forty-eight hours to decide if a news story had been written "in bad faith." If so, it could be blocked.

Opponents of the bills have argued that the proposed laws amount to an attack on free expression. It might also put a journalist's anonymous sources in danger or might prevent potential sources for stories from coming forward. Critics expressed fears that it might result in the creation of a "thought police" who would dictate what was and was not true. This, in turn, led to further questions: Who would decide whether something was true? Wouldn't such decisions be subject to that person's own bias and manipulation?

In July 2018, the lower house of the French parliament passed the new laws. However, when the bills advanced to the French Senate, they were quickly rejected.

Like France, Germany has also taken steps to control the rise of fake news after false rumors spread about Chancellor Angela Merkel.

The Role of Propaganda in Brexit

In June 2016, the people of Great Britain went to the polls. The issue to decide was whether to leave the European Union (EU), which the nation had joined in 1973. When the votes were tallied, 52 percent had chosen to leave. The decision is better known as Brexit. Yet within days, many people were regretting their votes

Anti-immigrant and anti-EU propaganda played a huge role in the UK's 2016 Brexit campaign. Almost immediately after the results were announced, many voters claimed they had been misled.

as they discovered the massive role that propaganda had played in the highly divisive Brexit campaign.

Brexit was heavily promoted by a number of scare tactics that included promises of billions more for the National Health Service (the United Kingdom's public health service) upon leaving the EU. Immediately after the results were announced, chief campaigners admitted this was not true.

Darker propaganda focused on immigration. Reports spoke of swarms of migrants coming ashore at Dover, England, while ignoring the fact that the rise in net migration figures was actually caused by fewer British people moving overseas. This also carried a racist undertone as billboards showed thousands of brown-skinned people supposedly attempting to enter the country.

Despite the factual inaccuracies, the campaign was hugely successful, playing upon the public's fears of a rise in terrorism. Yet the violence came in another form. Within one week of the Brexit vote, hate crimes in the United Kingdom increased by 500 percent.

Germany

France is not the only European nation battling fake news. Germany adopted a law in 2017 that sought to end the posting of hate speech and false information on social media. Outlets that published such information would face heavy fines. As additional punishment, company directors might also face individual fines. The new law was largely in response to the rise of fake news the year before. While campaigning for reelection, German chancellor Angela Merkel faced false claims that she was the daughter of Adolf Hitler and that she had once been a member of the Stasi, East Germany's brutal secret police.

Fake news reached a fever pitch in Germany in 2016 when a story emerged claiming that a thirteen-year-old Russian girl had been attacked by Middle Eastern refugees. The Berlin police soon proved that the story was a fake, but it had already been shared widely on both Russian and German media. Protest marches were held, encouraged by far-right and anti-migrant groups. Many in the government believed that the IRA or another Russian group had planted the story in an attempt to discredit Merkel and to lessen her chances of reelection. The German law was passed, but like the proposed French law, it has been strongly criticized as threatening free speech and the freedom of the press.

Legislating Truth

Laws limiting fake news in Germany are a sharp contrast to the policies of the United States. The First Amendment to the US Constitution protects fake news and propaganda with only a few

Germany's strict laws banning the Nazi flag and memorabilia are in sharp contrast to the First Amendment protections of free speech in the United States.

Julian Assange Speaks About Fake News

Wikileaks founder Julian Assange has been a vocal supporter of fake news. He argues that it helps us to become more critical of what we read in the mainstream media.

One person who has been quick to speak out in favor of the growing awareness of fake news is WikiLeaks founder Julian Assange.

Assange has been a vocal critic of the media, calling it "one of the most destructive forces to have ever existed." During a 2017 debate about fake news, he said that in all major wars since and including the Second World War, the public and troops have been mobilized by media lies, and therefore, they are responsible for thousands of deaths.

In contrast, he argues that WikiLeaks is a source of pure information, an "intellectual treasure." Since it is pure, unfiltered information, he claims that it has no political agenda and cannot hurt anyone. He says, "Information very, very rarely is dangerous."

The conversation about fake news is something Assange views as a positive because he argues it is drawing attention to the fact that so much media is manipulated to suit a certain bias. Speaking at one conference, he told the audience to "ground your debate about fake news in the reality that news has always been fake."

Assange's critics would argue that he, too, manipulates information by deciding what to make public and when to do so.

exceptions. Although freedom of the press is valued in Europe, after the Second World War, many individual nations enacted some laws that would be unconstitutional in the United States. For example, both France and Germany have laws forbidding the display of Nazi symbols. Making laws to stop fake news is understandable. After all, Europe has seen first hand how propaganda can be abused to incite violence and war. However, the risk is that such laws are similar to laws that might be used to silence the media in more authoritarian nations. At what point do laws violate a person's freedom of speech?

Another point for discussion is who is allowed to determine what is true and what is fake for the sake of laws? At first, the answer seems obvious. Major newspapers and magazines typically hire fact-checkers whose job is to verify claims, quotes, statistics, and so on. However, even this role could be met with claims of bias if a fact-checker were working for the courts or the government. Furthermore, if it is up to a government and the ruling party to decide what is fake and therefore what should be banned, democracy would be at severe risk.

Laws against fake news have been proposed in a number of countries, including Australia, Italy, and Brazil. Opponents of these laws make arguments along the lines of the First Amendment in the United States. They say that freedom of speech should be upheld and that censorship can be a slippery slope even if it starts with good intentions. They argue instead that the best way to fight fake news and propaganda is through self-governance. Readers should take it upon themselves to remain informed and to critically think about what they read or see. At the same time, media sources should take more care in what they publish and broadcast.

On the other hand, people who support the proposed laws against fake news argue that we cannot depend on people and organizations to self-govern. They say that the misuse of information is threatening democracy. They believe that media companies value profits and the collection of personal data (that they can then sell) more than they value shielding consumers from fake news. Therefore, they say that laws may be the only way to bring about results. Even so, they agree with opponents of censorship in one important respect: that the public must educate themselves and evaluate media more critically to become informed citizens. A truly democratic society depends upon education and information being accessible to all.

SUPPORT
FREE
PRESS!
eople for
ee Press
FACTS MATTER
People for
Free Press
DIVERSE

CHAPTER 4

The Power of the People and the Press

A number of new initiatives are attempting to beat fake news and to restore the reputation of journalism. These efforts can help democracies thrive. After all, access to real news helps voters make informed decisions.

Support for Journalism

In April 2017, the billionaire Pierre Omidyar, founder of eBay, announced that he was creating a foundation to fund investigative reporting. In total, he has promised to give $100 million in grants to organizations around the world. Omidyar said, "The $100 million will be dedicated to supporting independent media, tackling misinformation and hate speech, and looking at ways in which technology can help repair relationships between citizens and government." Some of the first recipients of funding grants were the International Consortium of Investigative Journalists and the Anti-Defamation League.

Opposite: Various rallies have been held, such as this one in New York, to protest President Donald Trump's self-proclaimed war on the media.

Omidyar has not been alone in taking action. PEN International, an organization that promotes writers and freedom of expression, has created a series of reports calling for education. They have emphasized the importance of media literacy as a skill to be taught in schools. It is up to everyone, they say, to play their part in ensuring the accuracy of the news. This includes journalists, who must follow proper ethical practices and news outlets that must publish diverse voices and expose fake news. In the realm of social media, Google, YouTube, Facebook, and Twitter have all announced that they are dedicating large amounts of money to rooting out false accounts set up by members of the IRA and to halting the spread of harmful fake news.

One initiative that has been a little more controversial is PropOrNot, which bills itself as "your friendly neighborhood propaganda identification service." PropOrNot claims to be a group of American citizens from different backgrounds who volunteer their time to identify harmful Russian propaganda. Through their website, they put together a list of outlets that regularly publish what they conclude to be propaganda. At first glance, their goal appears to be admirable and well-intentioned: educating the public. However, some journalists have raised concerns for several reasons. The group is entirely anonymous, prompting some people to ask how they can be transparent in exposing propaganda while keeping their own identities hidden. Other concerns have been raised about what media sources are placed on their list and why. While many on the list are as expected, some seemingly reputable publications have been named with no explanation.

Sadly, the rise in fake news has come at a time when many newspapers have made drastic changes to their editing and fact-checking departments due to budget cuts. In the past decade, many

The *Washington Post* attracted attention in early 2017 when the newspaper changed its slogan to "Democracy Dies in Darkness." The slogan is a reminder that trustworthy journalism is essential.

How Does Facebook Help to Spread or Stop Fake News?

Facebook CEO Mark Zuckerberg testified before Congress in 2018 at hearings about social media's role in influencing elections through the spread of fake news.

One online outlet that has generated a lot of criticism for its role in the spread of fake news and political propaganda is Facebook. Because it is so easy to share a story with the click of a button, fake stories are able to go viral in a matter of minutes, with most people never looking beyond the sensationalistic headline and an eye-catching image.

After the 2016 presidential election, Facebook was one of several social media platforms accused of spreading fake news and propaganda to help sway the results. At first, the company denied this. However, in 2017, they admitted to finding that bots (automated accounts) based in Russia had bought large amounts of advertising and had used that to spread falsehoods.

Since then, Facebook has been working to find a way to deal with the spread of fake news while still providing a platform that embraces freedom. They have employed an army of fact-checkers, and in July 2018, they announced that they would remove any fake stories that seemed to promote violence. All other fake news stories would be allowed to remain. The company said that this would "strike the right balance between free expression and a safe and authentic community."

Whether it works remains to be seen, but it is likely that technology and social media will be struggling with this issue for some time to come.

newspapers have reduced their staff. However, most of the major publications, like the Associated Press, NPR, the *Washington Post*, and the *New York Times* still have in-house fact-checking teams. The BBC has gone one step further in response to fake news allegations. In 2017, they set up a new department whose entire purpose is to investigate, fact-check, and debunk falsehoods.

Young People Take a Stand

Protecting and ensuring a healthy democracy depends not just on voting but on taking an active interest in issues and speaking out when necessary. The history of the United States is filled with examples of protest. Protesters have been instrumental in bringing about an end to the Vietnam War, in fighting for LGBT rights, and in the civil rights movement. At the heart of these protests are young people. The move to educate and fight back against fake news is no different. Programs at schools can help to inform students of all ages.

The National Association for Media Literacy Education is behind some programs that help students evaluate the news. The organization provides a student-led blog where recent topics include tips on understanding news headlines and responding to claims by President Trump about fake news.

Some young activists have found themselves the target of fake news and propaganda. Students from Florida's Parkland High School have become active in various political movements since the mass shooting at their school in February 2018. Although not directly fighting fake news, they have found themselves targeted in many false news stories as a result of their campaigning for gun control and against violence. Examples include the false image of Emma Gonzalez tearing up a copy of the US Constitution. In reality, she was tearing up a paper target. The false image went viral, causing

Student activists, such as Parkland survivor Emma Gonzalez, have frequently found themselves the targets of fake news stories designed to discredit them.

Several organizations are creating educational programs to help students learn how to read news stories critically and to be aware of possible propaganda.

Supreme Court justice Louis Brandeis believed freedom of speech means there will always be false stories, but the solution is "more speech." It is up to citizens to separate fact and fiction.

a number of threats to be made against her. She and her colleagues have continued to fight back against such negative propaganda campaigns by speaking out. They have encouraged others to continue to protest and to call attention to intentional lies when they see them. In doing so, they continue to pursue the democratic concept of free speech and free expression.

Fake news is not illegal. Neither is propaganda. There are some exceptions, of course, such as if they make libelous or defaming claims. Yet for the most part, even the most obviously false claims are protected by a constitutional right to free speech. This means that the government may not prohibit or censor them. However, it does not prevent us, the public consumer, from taking an active role in stopping the spread of such stories. Even if protected by law, something can still be a threat to democracy. While a satirical piece of entertainment can be harmless, other pieces may deliberately seek to cause harm or to discourage people from voting.

Furthermore, the constant flood of fake news undermines the very freedom of speech that allows it to exist. It does so by undermining our access to information. Already, too many people assume that much of the news is fake and so there is no reason to believe any of it. They stop attempting to inform themselves.

It is essential that the public, the media, and the government all take steps to combat the problem. However, whatever steps are taken must not become a bigger problem. As we have seen with proposed laws in France and other countries, enforcing laws about what is and is not true may create just as much of a risk to democracy as the very targets of the laws. To paraphrase the advice of Supreme Court justice Louis Brandeis, the best weapons against fake news and propaganda are more speech and an educated citizenry.

Tips for Identifying Fake News

Washington Post reporters Barton Gellman (*left*) and Eli Saslow (*right*) are applauded by their colleagues in 2014 after both receiving Pulitzer Prizes for excellence in journalism.

In this era of fake news, it is increasingly important for people to remain aware and informed. We need to be able to decide if a story is truly fake news or if it has been labeled that way to discredit it. There are several steps that readers can take to be media literate.

When looking at a story, whether in a newspaper, online, or on television, ask a few questions. First, consider the headline. These are often designed to manipulate and mislead, and many outlets assume people will never read beyond this. If it seems too outrageous, it probably is. Always read beyond the headline. The "meat" of the story may provide a very different version of events. Check to see who wrote the story and who published it. Is it an outlet with a reputation of fairness? How many outlets are publishing the story? The idea of a story that no one else has discovered is very attractive, but the reality is that with modern technology, most stories spread quickly. What outlets are reporting the story, and are they actually reporting it themselves, or simply copying one unverified source? Lastly, what sources and facts are cited? Look for statistics and experts that you can verify.

In following these steps, we can be informed readers and therefore informed citizens. That is one of the best ways to protect a democracy.

GLOSSARY

benign Not harmful.

bias A prejudice or favoritism of one person, group, or opinion over another.

Brexit An abbreviated form of "British exit" used to refer to the proposed exit of the United Kingdom from membership in the European Union.

censorship The prohibition or banning of material that is believed to be unsuitable for some reason.

citizen journalism Reporting done by everyday people.

debunk To expose as being false.

defamation False statements that hurt someone's reputation.

democracy A political system where citizens have a voice through the election of representatives.

disinformation False information that is spread on purpose.

fake news An item of news that can be proven to be false. The phrase has also come to refer to an unfavorable or critical news item.

hoax A story meant to trick readers or viewers.

incite To stir up violence.

libel Published text that is false and hurts someone's reputation.

media literacy The ability to analyze news and media in all forms, including print articles, television shows, advertisements, and radio programs.

partisan Biased in favor of a particular political party or cause.

propaganda A form of fake news that is intentionally designed to manipulate people's emotions or to sway their opinion.

satire A form of humor that typically exaggerates or ridicules as a way of exposing stupidity.

sound bite A short phrase or saying, usually from an interview, which is given as an example of the larger whole.

spin To present information or a news story so that it is received in a positive way.

upheaval Extreme change or disruption.

FURTHER INFORMATION

Books

Connolly, Sean. *Political Messages and Propaganda.* Getting the Message. Ontario, Canada: Smart Apple Media, 2009.

Hand, Carol. *Everything You Need to Know about Fake News and Propaganda.* The Need to Know Library. New York: Rosen Publishing, 2018.

New York Times Editorial Staff. *Fake News: Read All About It.* In the Headlines. New York: Rosen Publishing, 2019.

Websites

FactCheck.org

https://www.factcheck.org

This nonpartisan organization monitors political news, interviews, and advertising and checks for accuracy. Their website also provides fact-checking reports on science and health news.

International Programme for the Development of Communication

https://en.unesco.org/programme/ipdc

Part of UNESCO, the IPDC was originally established to help support a free press in developing countries. It now also provides education and resources about fighting fake news.

PEN America

https://pen.org

PEN America works to defend freedom of speech and press around the world through advocacy and education. Get updates about issues affecting journalism on this site.

Videos

How False News Can Spread: Noah Tavlin

https://www.youtube.com/watch?v=cSKGa_7XJkg&t=138s

TED-Ed producer Noah Tavlin explains why fake news travels so fast.

How to Spot Fake News

https://www.youtube.com/watch?v=AkwWcHekMdo

Learn to identify fake news for yourself.

BIBLIOGRAPHY

Allcot, Hunt, and Matthew Gentzkow. *Social Media and Fake News in the 2016 Election*. Cambridge, MA: National Bureau of Economic Research, 2017.

Attkisson, Sharyl. *The Smear: How Shady Political Operatives and Fake News Control What You See, What You Think, and How You Vote*. New York: Harper Collins, 2017.

Babiracki, Patrick. "Why Americans Keep Falling for Russian Propaganda." *Washington Post*, September 13, 2017. https://www.washingtonpost.com/news/made-by-history/wp/2017/09/13/why-americans-keep-falling-for-russian-propaganda/?utm_term=.1b42ea548699.

Barclay, Donald A. *Fake News, Propaganda, and Plain Old Lies*. London, UK: Rowman & Littlefield, 2018.

Chertoff, Michael. "Fake News and the First Amendment." Harvard Law Review, November 10, 2017. https://blog.harvardlawreview.org/156-2.

Cohen, Nick. "The British Right's Propaganda Is an Affront to Democracy." *Guardian*, October 14, 2017. https://www.theguardian.com/commentisfree/2017/oct/14/british-rights-propaganda-is-an-affront-to-democracy-brexit.

De Botton, Alain. *The News: A User's Manual.* New York: Pantheon, 2014.

Drainville, Ray. "The Visual Propaganda of the Brexit Leave Campaign." Hyperallergic, July 12, 2016. https://hyperallergic.com/310631/the-visual-propaganda-of-the-brexit-leave-campaign.

Herold, Benjamin. "Media Literacy vs. Bogus News." *Education Week* 36, no. 15 (2016): 12–13.

Jackson, Pamela Taylor, and James Ronald Stanfield. "The Role of the Press in a Democracy: Heterodox Economics and the Propaganda Model." *Journal of Economic Issues* 38, no. 2 (2004): 475–482.

Nossel, Suzanne. "The Pro-Free Speech Way to Fight Fake News." *Foreign Policy*, October 12, 2017. https://foreignpolicy.com/2017/10/12/the-pro-free-speech-way-to-fight-fake-news.

Page, Clarence. "Does the First Amendment Protect Fake News?" *Chicago Tribune*, December 6, 2016. http://www.chicagotribune.com/news/opinion/page/ct-pizzagate-fake-news-first-amendment-perspec-1207-20161206-story.html.

Redmond, Pearse. "The Historical Roots of CIA-Hollywood Propaganda." *American Journal of Economics and Sociology* 76, no. 2 (2017).

Rutenberg, Jim. "Media's Next Challenge: Overcoming the Threat of Fake News." *New York Times*, November 6, 2016. https://www.nytimes.com/2016/11/07/business/media/medias-next-challenge-overcoming-the-threat-of-fake-news.html.

Shafer, Jack. "Pravda on the Checkout Line." *Politico*, February 2017. https://www.*politico*.com/magazine/story/2017/01/tabloid-newspapers-trump-media-propaganda-214627.

Shpancer, Noam. "The Con of Propaganda." *Psychology Today*, February 15, 2017. https://www.psychologytoday.com/us/blog/insight-therapy/201702/the-con-propaganda.

Siddiqui, Sabrina, and David Smith Washington. "Trump's Attacks on Media Raise Threat of Violence Against Reporters, UN Experts Warn." *Guardian*, August 2, 2018.

Stanley, Jason. *How Propaganda Works*. Princeton, NJ: Princeton University Press, 2015.

Tattershall, Ian, and Peter Nevraumont. *Hoax: A History of Deception*. New York: Black Dog & Leventhal, 2018.

Tharoor, Ishan. "'Fake News' and the Trumpian Threat to Democracy." *Washington Post*, February 7, 2018. https://www.washingtonpost.com/news/worldviews/wp/2018/02/07/fake-news-and-the-trumpian-threat-to-democracy/?utm_term=.0f059a9466db.

Washington, Lindsey. "Fake News; Real Politics." *Diplomatic Courier*, April 10, 2018. https://www.diplomaticcourier.com/2018/04/10/fake-news-real-politics.

Wood, Allen. "Propaganda and Democracy." *Theoria* 31, no. 3 (2016): 381–394.

INDEX

Fiona Young-Brown has written a number of books for middle school and high school students, including *Edward Snowden: NSA Contractor and Whistle-Blower* and *News Literacy: Seeing Through Internet Hoaxes*. She has also authored several books about the history of Kentucky and enjoys writing about a wide variety of topics, including food, travel, and great apes. Originally from England, Young-Brown now lives in Lexington, Kentucky, with her husband and dog.